ANCIENT CIVILIZATIONS

THE
PHOENICIANS
MYSTERIOUS SEA PEOPLE

by
KATHERINE REECE

Rourke
Publishing LLC
Vero Beach, Florida 32964

www.rourkepublishing.com

PHOTO CREDITS:
Courtesy Charles Penny, www.sobi.org: pages 33, 38; Courtesy Charles Reasoner: pages 24, 30, 31, 35; Courtesy www.freestockphotos.com: pages 4, 17, 28, 37; Courtesy Lebanese Global Information Center, www.lgic.org: pages 9, 12; Courtesy Library of Congress, Prints and Photographs Division: page 28; Courtesy NASA: pages 5, 7, 42; Courtesy Peter Brown: pages 10, 13, 25, 40, 42; Courtesy Rohm Padilla: pages 15, 27, 32, 44; Courtesy Salim G. Khalaf, www.phoenicia.org, A Bequest Unearthed: page 26;

DESIGN AND LAYOUT: ROHM PADILLA

Library of Congress Cataloging-in-Publication Data

Reece, Katherine E., 1955-
  The Phoenicians : the mysterious sea people / Katherine Reece.
      p. cm. --   (Ancient civilizations)
Includes bibliographical references and index.
ISBN 1-59515-236-9 (hardcover)
  1. Phoenicians--Juvenile literature.   I. Title. II. Series: Reece,
Katherine E.,   1955-   Ancient civilizations.
   DS81.R36 2004
   939'.44--dc22
                              2004012012

TITLE PAGE IMAGE
A view of the sun setting on the Mediterranean Sea
from the coast of what was Ancient Phoenicia

TABLE OF CONTENTS

INTRODUCTION

As you look at the words on this page and read the print, do you wonder how the alphabet you use came to exist? Did you realize that you could be looking at scribbles or pictures instead of letters to represent the words and sounds you use if some civilization in time had not changed and improved how we write? Why was there a need to do so? When you pick up food at the local grocery store, have you thought about how the item got to your store from other regions or even distant lands? Who first started trade and commerce between distant countries? How did sailors first learn to navigate the open seas?

This clay face is the lid to a burial coffin. It is from Canaan, an area south of modern Lebanon.

Phoenicia was located along the coast of the Mediterranean Sea and was centered in modern Lebanon. This photo is of the Dead Sea in the south to the Gulf of Iskenderun at the top of the photo. The Sea of Galilee lies in between, and north of that is modern Lebanon.

PHOENICIA

SEA OF GALILEE

PALESTINE

DEAD SEA

CANAAN

Little is known about the **origins** of Phoenicians (fo NEE shuns), but this group of traders are remembered for their enormous role in our world today. They carried knowledge from the Mediterranean Sea to the west. Their powerful ships served as models for their enemies. They influenced the evolution of the alphabet we use today. Because of the design of the land where they lived, they were forced to look to the sea as their outlet to the world around them. Located between the two great, evolving ancient cultures of Egypt and Mesopotamia, the Phoenicians were politically dominated throughout much of their history. Yet, these same connections enabled a cultural exchange of ideas between diverse groups of peoples.

Powerful sailing ships carried Phoenician goods and knowledge to remote parts of the ancient world. Phoenicians had a large influence on the modern world thanks to their boats that traveled far.

CHAPTER 1:
WHERE WAS PHOENICIA?

Squeezed between tree-covered mountains to the east and the Mediterranean Sea to the west in an area not much larger than the state of Connecticut, an ancient civilization evolved in what was then the center of the ancient world. Phoenicia comes from the Greek word, **phoinix**, meaning "red-purple" and later referred to the people who traded the goods from the area. Phoenicia was actually the northern portion of a region known as **Canaan**. Canaan included present-day Lebanon in the north, parts of modern Syria and Jordan, Israel, and Palestine. Three ancient peoples occupied this area. There were the **Philistines** on the southern section of the coast, the **Israelites** in villages on the hills, and the Phoenicians who created their own **empire** in the north end of this coastal strip.

The area known as Phoenicia was centered in and around modern Lebanon.

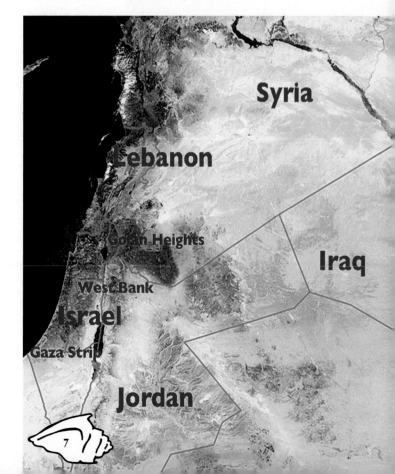

Syria

Lebanon

Golan Heights

Iraq

West Bank

Israel

Gaza Strip

Jordan

MIGRATION OF NOMADS

Nomads from the desert areas such as the Sinai in Egypt and the Arabian Desert to the east may have migrated north and west in search of water and food. As they moved northwest along the mountains, there was a mountain pass that led them westward to the sea coast.

During the 3500s **B.C.E.**, ancient civilizations were developing along the Nile River in Egypt and the **Fertile Crescent** in **Mesopotamia.** In their search for water and food, **nomads** from barren, desert areas were drawn to the rich, fertile river valleys of the Nile, the **Tigris and Euphrates** river basin, and the lands on the eastern shores of the Mediterranean Sea. In their westward migration, small numbers stayed along the coast and made homes for themselves.

Early Phoenicians were migrating nomads in search of food and water.

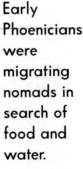

Phoenicia, or modern-day **Lebanon**, is divided into four main regions that run north to south and **parallel** to the Mediterranean Sea. Within a mile or two from the beaches are snow-capped mountains that rise to an altitude of 3,300 feet (1,000 m). Rarely more than one mile (1.5 km) wide, the fertile coastal plain is broken by the foothills of the Lebanon Mountains. It was along this coastal plain that the Phoenicians' prosperous cities grew.

There are two chains of mountains called the Lebanon Mountains and Anti-Lebanon Mountains with the Bekaa Valley in between. The Lebanon mountain chain contains many rivers that flow westward to the sea. Its highest peak is 10,138 feet (3,090 m). Behind the Lebanon Mountains is the 9.3 mile- (15 km-) wide Bekaa Valley. The Litani and Orontes rivers irrigate this valley and provide water for crops.

Snow-capped mountains of Lebanon give water runoff to the mild climates and communities that surround them.

An **arid** mountain mass called the Anti-Lebanon Mountains forms the boundary with present-day Syria. Actually, this is a cluster of three peaks with the highest being 9,200 feet (2,804 m) above sea level. Called Sirion by the ancient Sidonians and Mt. Hermon today, this peak is covered with snow most of the year. Runoff from this snow-covered mountain's western and southern slopes feeds several streams and rivers that merge to become the Jordan River.

The Mediterranean climate of Phoenicia ranged from hot, dry summers to cool, rainy winters. Daytime temperatures averaged around 86°F (30°C) with the nights slightly lower.

Winter temperatures on the coast were usually 59°F (15°C), but days might be dry and mild one day and wet and chilly the next. Summer mountain temperatures might be as high as 78.8°F (26°C) with cool nights. The higher elevations were cold and snowy in the winter.

The sun setting at the port of Byblos

CHAPTER II:

WHO WERE THE PHOENICIANS?

The Phoenicians were truly one of the great peoples of the ancient world. They were sailors, **navigators**, and traders who were the first to send explorers to establish cities throughout the Mediterranean Sea area. They traveled all the way to the **Strait of Gibraltar**, sailed around Africa and as far as western Europe. While the Phoenicians may not have invented the alphabet, we know they were the carriers of this knowledge to regions near and far. The Phoenicians themselves left few records behind, but Greek and Roman historians tell us of their seamanship and shrewd business dealings.

The ancient Phoenicians were protected by mountains to the east, had access to a rich fertile land for crops, could fish in the sea, and hunt wildlife in the mountains. The earliest settlers in this region most likely came from the Arabian Peninsula to the southwest around 3200 B.C.E. They formed a loose **federation** of **city-states** on the narrow coastal strip. The main cities were Byblos, Tyre, Sidon, Berytus, and Arwad. It was only natural for the Phoenicians to look to the sea, and the rocky foothills provided excellent harbors for shipbuilding and trade.

Each city-state had its own king and fleet of ships. Phoenician city-states were never united into a single country. The king of a city-state ruled along with a council of elders selected from a privileged group of citizens. These government officials were called **shofets.**

Tyre and Arwad actually stood on islands offshore. Berytus is now Beirut, the present capital of Lebanon. The early nomadic immigrants to Byblos must have truly felt that the land would provide for all their needs. Instead of a flat plateau, the steep mountain slopes were covered with forests of fir, cypress, and cedar trees. Instead of dry water holes, there were clear mountain streams. Rather than barren land, the fertile fields supported gardens of figs and olives. Mountain goats, wild sheep, and panthers were in abundance for hunting.

(Above) figs grew abundantly in the temperate climate of much of Phoenicia.
(Left) warm inland areas such as the Bekaa Valley are irrigated by rivers and have rich farmlands.

CITY OF TYRE

Tyre was built on a small, rocky island off the coast and became a major seaport. Because access was only by water, it was protected from invasion until Alexander the Great built a raised way across the water, or causeway, to reach the island. This took seven years, but he finally conquered the Phoenicians.

(Left) ruins of the ancient city of Tyre

The earliest Phoenicians had limited shipbuilding abilities and sailed only in flat-bottomed barges along the shore. They became traders, but Egypt and Mesopotamia–who were more powerful neighbors–controlled the trade routes. Unlike other civilizations that sought power by building strong, fortified cities and acquiring large amounts of land, the Phoenicians devoted their time and energy to building better **keel**-hulled boats and sailing the open seas. Phoenicia became a wealthy **commercial** center because of its location near the sea, which provided a link between developing ancient civilizations.

Phoenicians needed a quick and easy way to keep records in shipping and trade. Their language was similar to their neighbors in Mesopotamia, and they were familiar with the **cuneiform** script. However, they thought writing with the wedge-shaped characters was too slow and clumsy. The Egyptians used **hieroglyphics** to draw small pictures of what was being described, and each picture represented the first sound of a word. To the Phoenicians, drawing these pictures took too much time even if shortened to scribbles.

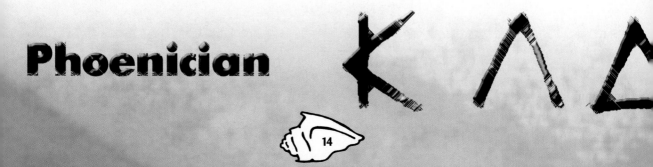

Phoenician

Modern Roman	A	G	D	E	Z	H	O	P	S
Early Latin	A	C	D	E	Z	H	O	Γ	S
Greek	Δ	Γ	Δ	E	Z	B	O	Π	Σ
Phoenician	K	Λ	Δ	E	I	B	O	1	W

This table shows how the modern Roman alphabet finds much of its roots in the original Phoenician alphabet, which consisted of 22 letters.

The Phoenicians quickly adapted these earliest forms of writing and developed a new system where sounds of the voice were represented by letters or a combination of letters. They had an alphabet of 22 consonant letters. Later the Greeks added vowel sounds, which completed the English alphabet that we use today. In their sea trade, Phoenicians are credited with being "carriers of civilization," since they spread this new alphabet to many places.

CHAPTER III:

FOOD, CROPS, AND ANIMALS

With rivers for irrigation, the Phoenicians could grow a wide assortment of crops for their use, as well as for trade. Fruits and vegetables included apples, melons, citrus fruits, grapes, wheat, and olives. Sheep and goats that grazed the mountain slopes were raised for their milk and meat. The variety of game to hunt in the mountains included panthers, bears, gazelles, and wild sheep.

(Right) crops like apples, which Phoenicians grew for themselves, were also traded abroad. (Below) gazelles were some of the wild game that roamed the area.

Grapes were used to make wine. Wine was a local beverage, but it was also exported. In addition, the wine was used to preserve meat and fish for shipment. Oils made from olives or cedar trees were valued and shipped in large clay jars with painted bottoms called **amphorae.**

(Above) wine was made from grapes that were grown in irrigated fields. (Left) the wine was then stored in clay jars and shipped abroad along with other exports like fish (below).

While they were able to grow and export a variety of crops, agriculture was never the main reason for the Phoenicians' **prosperity**. Their most valuable resource was the forests that grew on the nearby mountains. Cedars grew to heights of 131 feet (40 m) and measured 13 feet (4 m) around. Unlike the acacia and oil palms in Egypt with their crooked trunks, these cedars could be cut into long beams for building ships, houses, and temples. The fragrant oil from the cedar was used in Egypt for wrapping the bodies of **mummified** kings.

The cedars of Lebanon are still world famous and are seen today on the flag of Lebanon.

CHAPTER IV

WHAT DID THE PHOENICIANS WEAR?

(Above) early Phoenician settlers had a simple dress of a single wrap around the body or waist. (Far right) later the dress became more elaborate and decorative, and Phoenicians became known for their clothing.

Phoenician men and women wore ankle-length robes with fringed hems. Sometimes the robes for men stopped right below the knees, making them look more like **tunics** that they tied at the waist with a **sash.** Sleeves could be short, long, or elbow length. Wealthier individuals could afford embroidery or fancy weaving in their clothing.

DYES FROM SEA CREATURES

Thousands of sea snails were required to produce a single ounce of dye, so only the rich could afford it. The sea snails were gathered from shallow waters and left in pools of salt water to die and rot. Then they were removed from their shells and water was added to produce the dye. Different snails gave colors that ranged from a deep red to deep purple to a pale pink.

Color for dyes was made from tiny sea creatures similar to snails. These dyes were not only popular among the Phoenicians, but were also in high demand for trade. Dyes made from plants had a tendency to fade from washing and exposure to sunlight. The red or purple dye from Phoenicia stayed bright for a long time.

(This page and opposite) many different types of sea creatures were used by Phoenicians to make the different colors of dye.

20

The smell from rotting snails gave Sidon the reputation of having a very bad odor. Yet it was famous for the purple dye it produced. So rare and expensive was this dye that it became known as the color of royalty. Wearing clothes of this color was a sign of wealth and status in other lands. In fact, in Rome where the color appeared simply as a band around the hem of a **toga**, it was reserved for the elite by law.

Both men and women had their own unique hairstyles and headgear. Men's hair could be long, short, or sometimes curled. On their heads they wore a soft, peaked cap. Women's hair was worn long in back with bangs in front. Women's tall, rounded caps had veils that fell down their backs and alongside their faces.

In making their jewelry the Phoenicians learned from the Egyptians how to cast, hammer, and engrave metals such as gold, silver, and bronze. Only the wealthy could afford these gold and silver necklaces, pendants, earrings, bracelets, and rings. Poorer people may have worn less expensive bronze jewelry.

CHAPTER V:

TRADE WAS THE MAIN INTEREST

Phoenicians were seagoing traders from as early as 2900 B.C.E., with explorations that led to success and prosperity for their culture. By 1000 B.C.E., they had established trading colonies in distant regions such as Cyprus, Sicily, Sardinia, Africa, and Spain. Around 800 B.C.E. they founded the city of Carthage, which is part of the north African nation of Tunisia. The Phoenicians' interest in any region was based entirely on the products that could be bought and traded.

Early sailors traveled only during the day and kept the coast in sight.

At first, Phoenician sailors kept the coast in sight and only traveled by day so they would not become lost. Driven by a desire to expand their trade, these early sailors soon learned they could chart a course to distant lands by studying the stars and **constellations.** Ships followed the "Phoenician Star," or North Star, to exchange goods and spread ideas among cultures of the ancient world. The flickering stars at night became compass points to steer their course.

Once they learned how to chart stars, sailing at night became a possibility.

The city of Byblos became known for its shipbuilding. At first, small boats with the front or back shaped like a horse's head hugged the coastline to reach nearby regions of trade. These boats were called **Hippoi**, the Greek word for horses. Soldiers were used as **mariners** to protect the merchant fleets from pirates who would steal their valuable cargo.

Early ocean vessels were called Hippoi and had the front shaped like the head of a horse.

As navigational skills improved, and sailors could use the stars to guide them in open seas, they built larger trading boats, called **tubs.** Their deep, rounded hulls allowed for an entire lower deck of rowers with long-bladed oars that could move the boats rapidly through the water if no wind was present to fill their sails. The singular sail was shaped like a **trapezoid** and hung from a sturdy mast. **Brails** lowered and raised the sail. On the upper deck were cabins for ship commanders or passengers.

Phoenicians gained their reputation as people of the sea with superior shipbuilding skills.
(Right) a modern view of the port of Byblos. In ancient times it was well known for its shipbuilding.

The Phoenicians were masters in the export and import business. Not only did they prosper by trading for their own use, but they also acted as the middlemen for the exchange of goods among other lands. They used the raw materials from distant regions, borrowed and improved the manufacturing skills of various areas to create new products, and then traded them to areas in need.

Glass was also a popular export. Pictured is a head of a Phoenician man made out of glass beads.

Wine and oil produced in other lands was bottled in clay Phoenician jars and then sent abroad. Because the Middle East had little usable wood, Phoenician cedar with its fragrant aroma and straight trunks was prized for building. Cedar, pine, fine linen in beautiful colors, embroideries, metalwork, glass, wine, salt, oil, and dried fish became main exports.

(Right)
two major
exports of
Phoenicia were
purple cloth and
salt. The cloth was
famous worldwide,
and in Rome only
the wealthy were
allowed to wear
the color.

Phoenicians also
imported exotic
goods from abroad
such as
(right) horses, and
many spices like
(below) cinnamon.

(Below)
cedars from
Lebanon made
it to many
faraway lands.

At the height of their trading empire between 1000 and 800 B.C.E., the Phoenicians brought copper from Cyprus, linen from Egypt, silver, copper, and tin from Spain, Italy, and Turkey. Horses were imported from **Anatolia** and peacocks from Africa. Olive oil and wheat came from Israel. Gold could be found on ships that traveled to Spain and Africa. Among the list of other **exotic** imports were ostrich eggs, spices, incense, jewels, ivory, and **papyrus** for paper.

(Above) this panel of carved ivory was made by a Phoenician craftsworker.
(Bottom) many exotic items passed through ports such as Gibraltar.
(Bottom right) the Rock of Gibraltar

CHAPTER VI:

WAR AND CONQUEST OR COLONIZATION?

Each city-state in Phoenicia was independent and known for specific trade goods. At any given time one city-state might be wealthier than another, but the Phoenicians did not build their empire by conquering and controlling their neighbors or distant lands. Instead, their interest was to promote trade. This narrow coastal strip was a natural meeting place for a variety of cultures since it lay in the middle of traffic between Egypt, to the south, and Asia Minor and Mesopotamia, to the east.

The central location of Phoenicia caused the civilization to be dramatically influenced by outside cultures. These ruins at the city of Baalbek show the Roman influence on the city.

Yet, other cultures exercised control over Phoenicia throughout its history. These distant civilizations warred with each other in an effort to control trade routes and not lose access to the regions that had goods they needed. One civilization after another controlled Phoenicia by imposing taxes or making it one of their frontier colonies.

Egypt and Phoenicia both influenced each other culturally.

As early as 2686 B.C.E., Phoenicia exported its famed cedars to Egypt. By 2052 B.C.E. regular trade existed with timber and **pitch** going to Egypt in exchange for gold and manufactured goods. Phoenicia actually became a frontier province of Egypt in the 1400s B.C.E., and each country influenced the other. Phoenician nobles visited Egyptian courts and adopted their styles of clothing. At the same time, Phoenician religions affected the way Egyptians thought.

Mesopotamian influence is seen in the daily life of Phoenicians from the 1300s to 1200s B.C.E. The Phoenician elite of the cities wrote in cuneiform. Phoenicians sealed their documents with **cylinder seals.** Many of the tales of creation, the birth of gods, and the creation of human beings came to Phoenicia from Mesopotamia.

Map of the Mediterranean showing how far the Phoenician trade empire reached.

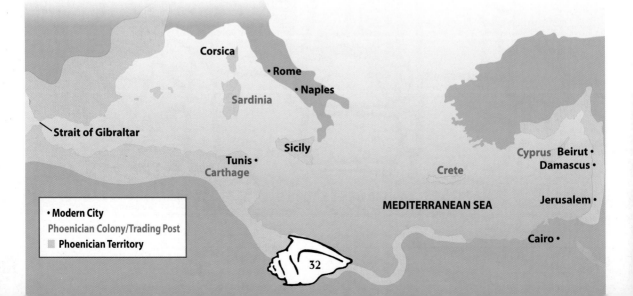

Corsica

• Rome

• Naples

Sardinia

Strait of Gibraltar

Sicily

Cyprus Beirut •

Tunis •

Damascus •

Carthage

Crete

Jerusalem •

MEDITERRANEAN SEA

• Modern City
Phoenician Colony/Trading Post
Phoenician Territory

Cairo •

From 1100 B.C.E., Phoenicians expanded their trade empire and built settlements on the island of Cyprus, the southern coast of Spain, the northern coast of Africa, and the western coast of Sicily. The people of Tyre founded the ancient city of Carthage, which was located where they could control trade from the eastern to the western Mediterranean Sea. These sea people ultimately controlled the Strait of Gibraltar, which gave them access to the Atlantic Ocean. Their trading **monopoly** now extended from western Africa to Europe. By the 600s B.C.E. they had sailed all the way around the tip of Africa and had even gone as far as what is now Cornwall in Britain.

TIN WAS VITAL

Tin and copper were the two metals needed to make bronze. The tin made the bronze harder so it would be useful in tools. Britain was the Phoenicians' secret source of tin. The name Britain may come from "barr" (land) and "tannic" (tin).

Shoreline near Carthage

An illustration of an Assyrian captive. Many Phoenicians were taken as slaves by conquering civilizations.

As ancient cultures sought to conquer and control one another, Phoenicia became one of the spoils of war. After the Mesopotamians came the Assyrians in 842 B.C.E. At first the Assyrians only demanded **tribute** or taxes from the Phoenician city-states, but by the 700s B.C.E., they made them a part of their empire. Hardship, revolt, and suppression followed for the next 250 years.

Assyria eventually fell to Babylonia in 612 B.C.E., and the Phoenician city-states once again prospered. The Babylonians used the experienced shipbuilders of Phoenicia to build and man their military fleets when Babylonia went to war with Persia. During the Persian wars, the entire Phoenician fleet came close to destruction. When the Persians finally defeated the Babylonians in 538 B.C.E., the Phoenicians once again flourished.

A Phoenician fleet heading into battle with the Greeks. The same skillful shipbuilding that made the Phoenician ocean ships famous was also employed by other civilizations, sometimes by force.

An illustration of Alexander the Great

The height of the Phoenician empire met its final decline in 332 B.C.E. when **Alexander the Great** from Greece conquered Tyre after an eight-month **siege.** Many Phoenicians were killed and others were sold into slavery. Over time the Greeks absorbed all that remained of the Phoenician culture.

Columns at Tyre show the Greek influence that came after being conquered by Alexander the Great.

CHAPTER VII:
BELIEFS AND GODS

Phoenicians were **polytheistic** and worshiped many gods and goddesses called Baal (lord) and Baalat (lady). While all the city-states identified and worshiped the same main god, local names varied. For instance, Melqart, the god of Tyre, was also known as the Baal of Tyre. The main gods of the Phoenicians were El, protector of the universe, and his son, Baal or Melqart. Melqart symbolized the annual growing seasons and was associated with the goddess Astarte, as she was known in Sidon. In Babylos, Astarte was called Baalat, our dear lady. Phoenicians prayed to Astarte to protect their children, give them good harvests, and maintain peace and harmony at home. Eshmum was the god of healing.

A statue of Baal, the main god of the Phoenician religion. He was depicted here holding a weapon, which is now missing.

Members of the city's royal family served as the most important priests in the temples. Large groups of people were needed to perform rituals, to prepare animals for sacrifice, and to entertain the gods and goddesses. These included priests, priestesses, servants, musicians, singers, dancers, barbers, butchers, and bakers.

Sacrifices were an important part of Phoenician religious beliefs. They felt that if the gods or goddesses were not happy, a ship might wreck on the seas, droughts could destroy crops, or they might be defeated in battle.

In order for things to go well, Phoenicians needed to perform many rituals and sacrifices for their gods. Animals were killed and other delicacies such as milk, wine, honey, fruit, or oil were offered. It is believed the Phoenicians also made human sacrifices to the gods, and for this they gained a reputation for cruelty.

HUMAN SACRIFICES?

Phoenicians are thought to have offered their children as sacrifices to Astarte or the goddess Tanit in exchange for protection in time of plague or war or as a favor from the gods. If the parent tried to fool the goddess by bringing a slave child, the goddess would be very angry and bring disaster to the city.

(Left) Carthage is a Phoenician burial site covered with stone containers and markers. It is thought this is the evidence of sacrifices made by the people to the gods.

CHAPTER VIII:

THE PEOPLE TODAY

Lebanese youths enjoying a game of basketball

Modern Lebanon now occupies the coastal strip once known as Phoenicia. This small country located east of the Mediterranean Sea and on the western edge of Asia has been a center for transportation, trade, and finance. Main cities include Beirut, Sidon, Tyre, and Tripoli. Approximately 3,439,000 people live in this small country with half of the population living around the Beirut area.

In the cities, life is much the same as you would expect to see in any modern country. The wealthy and middle-class citizens wear the same style of clothing as western nations. Restaurants serve a variety of dishes with bread, fruit, grains, meats and vegetables, and yogurt mixed with spices. People drink soft drinks, coffee, wine, and beer. Even though there is not a law requiring children to go to school, there are many public and private schools where parents send their children. There are also universities for higher education.

People enjoy literature, music, and art of both western and Lebanese cultures. The artistic creations in silverware, brassware, jewelry, needlework, and colorful glassware are similar to those of ancient times. People go to the beaches for relaxation and to enjoy water sports. They also play basketball, soccer, table tennis, and volleyball, and they ski in the snow-covered mountains.

An aerial view of the city of Beirut, the capital of modern Lebanon.

(Above) modern young Lebanese still fish the same spots on the coast of the Mediterranean Sea that their ancestors did.

(Below) Lebanon continues to export many of the country's products around the world such as electronics, chemicals, and wood products.

Poorer people live in rural areas or run-down sections of the cities. Their clothing is more traditional. The women wear colorful long dresses with ankle-length trousers. Men may be seen in multi-colored jackets and flowing headdresses.

Lebanon continues to be a center for manufacturing and agriculture. Cement, chemicals, electrical appliances, furniture, processed foods, and textiles are a few of the country's exports. Trade and banking rank as Lebanon's chief sources of income.

Those mysterious sea people known as the Phoenicians may have disappeared from civilization, but their contributions still exist in many cultures today. The Phoenicians borrowed most of their art, technology, and beliefs from others while learning and practicing various crafts until they outperformed their teachers. Their vast network of trade routes promoted exchange of ideas, customs, religious beliefs, crafts, and manufacturing skills. We are indebted to them for their role in "spreading" the contributions of one civilization to another.

A TIMELINE OF THE HISTORY
OF PHOENICIA

3200 B.C.E.	Nomadic settlers arrive in Phoenicia.
2900 B.C.E.	Phoenicians begin sea exploration and trade.
2750 B.C.E.	City of Tyre founded.
2686 B.C.E.	Trade between Egypt and Phoenicia for famed cedars.
2052 B.C.E.	Phoenicia exchanges cedars for Egyptian gold and manufactured goods.
1400 B.C.E.	Phoenicia is a frontier of Egypt.
1300 B.C.E.	Mesopotamian trade with Phoenicia established.

1100 B.C.E.	Phoenicia establishes independence; explorations reach Cyprus, the Coast of Spain, the northern Coast of Africa, and the western Coast of Sicily.
842 B.C.E.	Assyrians gain control over Phoenicia by conquering Mesopotamians.
700 B.C.E.	Phoenicia made a part of Assyrian Empire.
600 B.C.E.	Phoenicians sail as far as Britain.
612 B.C.E.	Babylonia conquers Assyria and gains control over Phoenicia.
538 B.C.E.	Persia defeats Babylonia.
332 B.C.E.	Alexander the Great conquers Tyre.

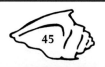

GLOSSARY

Alexander the Great - Greek warrior known for his many military conquests in the expansion of the Greek Empire.

Amphorae - Clay vessels used by Phoenicians for transporting food, grains, and oils.

Anatolia - The part of Turkey comprising the peninsula of Asia Minor.

Arid - Excessively dry, with not enough rainfall for crops to grow.

B.C.E. - "Before the Common Era," or before the year "1." This term is similar to using B.C., which refers to time before the birth of Christ. B.C.E. is a non-religious phrase for the same time period.

Brails - A rope used for hauling a sail up and down.

Canaan - An ancient region in southwestern Asia on the east coast of the Mediterranean Sea.

City-state - An independent state consisting of the city and surrounding land area.

Commercial - The exchange or buying and selling of large quantities of goods between areas involving transportation from place to place.

Constellations - An arrangement of a specific group of stars in the sky.

Cuneiform - A system of writing using "wedge-shaped" characters created by the ancient Sumerians.

Cylinder Seals - Seals first used in Mesopotamia to indicate that a message on a clay tablet was genuine or to indicate ownership of a possession. An image was carved deep in the surface, and when rolled and pressed into damp clay, it produced a raised image.

Empire - A collection of kingdoms under one powerful ruler.

Exotic - Mysteriously different or unusual; introduced from another country.

Federation - A union of political units that surrender authority to one central authority.

Fertile Crescent - A region of western Asia that is shaped like a quarter moon and covers present-day Iraq, Syria, Lebanon, and Israel.

Hieroglyphics - A system of writing mainly in pictorial characters.

Hippoi - Greek word meaning "horse."

Israelites - Natives or inhabitants of the northern kingdom of ancient Israel.

Keel - A chief structural member in the construction of a boat that extends down the length of the underside of the boat. This projection holds the boat steady in waves and rough seas.

Lebanon - Modern country located north of Israel on the coast of the Mediterranean Sea.

Mariners - People who navigate or assist in navigating a ship.

Mesopotamia - An area located between the Tigris and Euphrates rivers that is the site of the world's first civilization. The Greek word means "land between two rivers."

Monopoly - Exclusive control or possession of something.

Mummify - To treat a dead body so as to protect it from decay.

Navigator - One who sails, steers, or charts a course over water.

Nomads - people who move from place to place and have no fixed residence.

Origin - The point at which something begins.

Papyrus - A plant used by ancient Egyptians, Greeks, and Romans to make paper by cutting it in strips and pressing it flat.

Parallel - Running in the same direction at equal distance between.

Philistines - Ancient sea people who lived on the southern coast of Canaan.

Phoenicia - Ancient country in southwest Asia at the eastern end of the Mediterranean Sea in modern Lebanon.

Phoinix - Greek word meaning red-purple, which referred to the people who traded a special dye made from a snail.

Pitch - A resin obtained from evergreens.

Polytheistic - A belief in many gods and goddesses.

Prosperity - The condition of being successful or thriving as it relates to the production, distribution, and consumption of goods and services.

Sash - A band of material around the waist of a skirt or trousers.

Shofets - Government officials of the Phoenician city-states.

Siege - A persistent military attack.

Strait of Gibraltar - A passage between Spain and Africa connecting the Atlantic Ocean and the Mediterranean and only about 8 miles (12.8 km) wide at its narrowest point.

Tigris and Euphrates - The two rivers that begin in the Taurus Mountains and flow to the Persian Gulf.

Toga - A loose, outer garment worn by citizens of ancient Rome.

Trapezoid - A four-sided figure with only two sides parallel.

Tribute - Payment by one nation for protection by another.

Tubs - Name given to early boats such as the Phoenician boats for navigating the seas. These had deeply rounded hulls that kept the boats more stable in the ocean.

Tunic - Any of a variety of loose-fitting cloaks extending to the hips or knees.

Books of Interest

Broida, Marian. *Ancient Israelites and their Neighbors.* Chicago Review Press, 2003.

Daniel, Dr. Glyn. *The Phoenicians.* Frederick Praeger, Inc., 1962.

Menen, Aubrey. *Cities in the Sand.* The Dial Press, 1973.

Herm, Gerhard. *The Phoenicians, the Purple Empire of the Ancient World.* William Morrow and Company, Inc., 1975.

Web Sites

http://phoenicia.org/toc.html

http://www.museum.upenn.edu/Canaan/index.html

http://www.laa.org/tours/phoenicians.htm

http://www.mariner.org/age/phoenicians.html

INDEX

Katherine E. Reece is a native of Georgia, where she grew up in a small town located in the foothills of the Blue Ridge Mountains. She has traveled throughout the United States, Europe, Australia, and New Zealand. Katherine completed her Bachelor of Fine Arts with an emphasis in studio art at the University of Colorado in Boulder, Colorado, where she now resides. Her extensive studies in art history gives her an appreciation for all that can be learned about the culture, beliefs, and traditions of ancient civilizations from the architecture, artifacts, and recordings that have been preserved through the centuries.

Gloucester County
Library System